LAUREATE SERIES

MMO CD 3817
MMO Cass. 8037

MUSIC MINUS ONE
INTERMEDIATE
CONTEST SOLOS

T0067835

TUNING
Before the piano accompaniment begins you will hear four tuning notes, followed by a short scale and another tuning note. This will enable you to tune your instrument to the record.

COMPACT DISC PAGE AND BAND INFORMATION

MMO CD 3817
MMO Cass. 8037

LAUREATE SERIES CONTEST SOLOS
INTERMEDIATE LEVEL FOR TRUMPET, VOL. 3

DANCE OF THE BALLERINA

from "Petroushka"

Compact Disc
Band 1 - With Trumpet
Band 7 - Without Trumpet

IGOR STRAVINSKY
Trans. by Quinto Maganini

Cassette

Side A - Band 6 ♩ = 104 (2'56")

Allegro

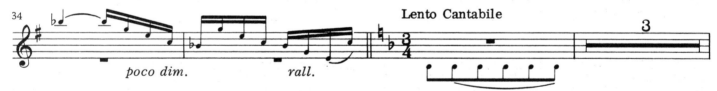

Lento Cantabile

MMO CD 3817
MMO Cass. 8037

PERFORMANCE GUIDE
COMMENTARY BY GERARD SCHWARZ

BALAY
Prelude et Ballade

This piece begins with very broad lines and florid passages thrown in as interjections. You should always be aware of what the piano is doing so that you can play with it easily. For example, the piano solo beginning in measure 13 is repeated in measure 48 with the trumpet. Don't let the sixteenth and thirty-second notes frighten you. There is no reason to rush; allow the scale passages a little freedom. Think *musically* rather than *mathematically!*

The Allegro must be very even with all attacks equal in intensity. Be careful not to cut slurred notes too short when they are followed by tongued notes. You might give a slight accent to the upper notes. The accompaniment beginning in measure 105 has a smooth delicacy which is marvelously effective. Do not accent the triplets. Work always for the long, broad line.

STRAVINSKY
Dance of the Ballerina from *Petroushka*

Every trumpet player should know this music; it is one of the major audition pieces for trumpet. This arrangement is taken from the cornet part in Stravinsky's 1911 version. It is not easy to get the correct notes in the slurred groups and the scales. Be very careful of your intonation in the section beginning at measure 40. Notes with a *portamento* marking, such as those in measure 43, are sometimes played too short. Play lyrically, and phrase with the accompaniment. Notice the marking in the Allegretto: *grazioso e poco grotesco* (graceful and a little grotesque). Work for a light, flexible feeling here. When the douplets begin in measure 102, you will need a very even attack. (In the 1946 version these douplets are triplets. It is important to know the different versions of this piece. Listen to several recordings and be aware of the changes that Stravinsky made).

GOEYENS
All 'Antica

The sub-title of this solo, "Concert Piece in the Olden Style," gives a true indication of how it should be performed. It must have the clarity and precision of the baroque period. Stress the downbeats, and do not let the ornaments dominate the phrases. You should play slight accents in measures 11 and 12. Be very careful to observe the sixteenth rests. Your entrances in measures 20 and 22 must not sound rushed. The trills should begin on the upper note and on the beat, to give the proper dissonance.

Measure 32 (written)

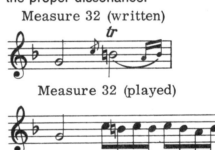

Measure 32 (played)

WHITNEY
Concertino for Trumpet — Third Movement

The last movement of Maurice Whitney's Concertino demands a good attack and facile articulation. It is most important to play the sixteenth note groups evenly; do not rush, even though the first two notes may be slurred. The downbeats must be emphasized. Otherwise the first notes in the phrase may sound like grace notes. The ascending figures beginning in measure 35 will be much easier if you add a slight crescendo leading up to the high note. The accompaniment begins a more lyric section at measure 71. When you enter in measure 85 you must keep the piano part in mind. Play measure 87 with a legato tongue on the eighths and triplets, even when they are marked *tenuto*. Accent the downbeats of measures 103 and 105 for good contrast. When you get to measure 127, you will need a very smooth slur. Study the rhythm, and be sure to differentiate between the quarter note triplets and the eighth-quarter-eighth note patterns. Notice the transition between short notes and legato beginning in measure 143. The sixteenth notes could be a little longer, to make a more musical line. From measure 214 you can surge ahead for a big, brilliant ending!

Gerard Schwarz

PRELUDE AND BALLADE

Compact Disc
Band 2 - With Trumpet
Band 8 - Without Trumpet

Cassette

Side B - Band 2 ♩ = 72 (5'09")

GUILLAUME BALAY

MMO CD 3817
MMO Cass. 8037

8

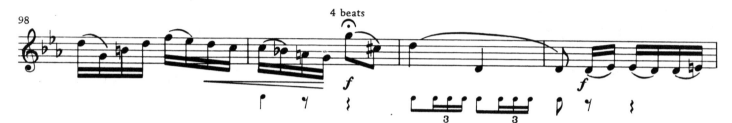

130

135

139

144 *retardéz* *plus lent*

151 *trés expressif*

157 Tempo I°

162

166

ALL'ANTICA

Concert Piece in the Olden Style

Compact Disc
Band 4 - With Trumpet
Band 11 - Without Trumpet

Cassette

Side B - Band 4 ♩ = 88 (3'47")

ALPHONSE GOEYENS (1894)

Moderato assai

MMO CD 3817
MMO Cass. 8037

CONCERTINO

Compact Disc
Band 5 - With Trumpet
Band 12 - Without Trumpet
Band 13 - Without Trumpet (Slow Version)

MAURICE C. WHITNEY

Cassette

Side B - Band 5 ♩ = 132 (3'36")
Side B - Band 6 ♩ = 100 (4'32").

Allegro scherzando

MMO CD 3817
MMO Cass. 8037

123

132

141

147

153

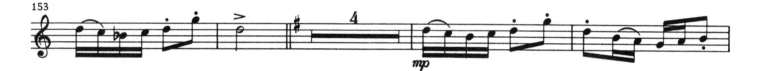

161

167

172

178

183

188

194

200

205

215

220

224

230

MMO CD 3817
MMO Cass. 8037

MUSIC MINUS ONE • 50 Executive Boulevard • Elmsford, New York 10523-1325